High Cut

My Model of No Criteria

Patricia Farrell

Leafe Press

Published by Leafe Press

www.leafepress.com

High Cut

My Model of No Criteria

for my mother

your invented and inventing hand
describes an inconsistent revolution
waltzing before
trying not to stick your finger in your eye
perhaps
thrown words
or things
is this
an arena
for displacements and lacunae
or is it just a garden swing
an intensified area of ink
whose mouth
as it shoots ball-bearings
we cannot see
we don't know how
it does this
we hear the percussion
certainly
if I push you hard enough
you will make a sound
standing back
no need to hug the paper
it is not your mother
in every part
from this
inside this
however small
the conversation carries on
like
in a speeded film
I am listening
the thing that makes the sound
is absent
replaced by scribbled lines
your feet
following on the sheet
a short hand
for fire and sudden noises
these are not
quite the right scribbles
in front of your head

with a parasol
arranging your hair
but if the furniture is at stake
the marks against your body
have something to do
with the sort
of insignificant moves
a hand's inclined to make
more heads more parasols
I can see
what is behind you
there is an empty space beyond your ear
testing
a new pen is a pleasure
it makes you feel good
a site of mutability
on the ground
a ruse used
revolving at high speed
in operation crashes
shoves our noses
into the discontinuous leaps
opening your mouth from head to foot
simply an explosion
you say
nothing
there is no point
at which to stop
not even if we close our eyes
write it off
or walk it out
inches from the front row
no bravado
almost a fait accompli
this time
is heavy and so
the boundaries are heavy
your frame immeasurable
this explosion of the body comes pretending
an enigmatic attitude
its parasols and chairs and tables
its fighter planes and flying figures

domestic detonation
discreetly to produce
the most rewarding lines of sight
gently tongue in cheek
terrain
percussive
rag-bags
how sad
without a tangent to lift yourself
not all the handsome people standing in the rain
can draw your outline
an acid black acrostic
tracing a description
of all empirical things
in the large expanse
of everything
I did not mean
you are raising your game
come on
position yourself sideways
underneath
for the tap dance
with its inundations of blood
your destiny like muslin
is revealing
remember how
in front of these strange men
who might think it is significant
that you are floating
tempting fate
a mouth without cheating
an excess of artificial skin
washed by the moon
on the page
and on a daily basis
our representatives
comfortably
obliterate
an amazing end to all amazing things
as everyone is traced
back to the first sorrow
to find those pensive lines

to recognize the planets
their hiding places
the constellations
a matrix of missing people
such as a footprint
left by the passage at night
of such glittering on hands and face
walking the well-dressed origins
think that over
for a while
seductions
I can't connect exactly
in the case of surfaces
and a moving point
which is not smooth
emits no sound
with which the air is
contact
when struck against it
to touch one another
in water touching
cannot be dry
thinking the moon lucid
plain
outward to the eye
upon the world
come all the sights
and sounds and smells of fear
and excited pleasure
the planes in the garden fail
to homogenize a gesture
the pilot rupturing to produce
a rose-bed
this lies beyond the set of pictures
embedded in the borders
the one you make is collage
we cannot go
back to it
back on it
the intonated deed
locution
listen to how you pronounce this

I do not love you
because you have twink'e toes
you have twinkle toes because I love you
we are
on delicate ground here
having an accent
in loaded terms they reverence
and float
until even I
start appealing
for a criterion
for my model of no criteria
the water which wets their bounding
placed on the surface of the eye the air possesses
mistakes an abstract air for shyness
the time it takes erratic globes once known to stray
there is no ironic contrast between
the garden furniture
and the military planes
war means elbow grease
so protect your patent leather shoes
you're a curious anomaly
in the simplified state
no margins
I can't dance with you if you're all laced-up
I saw you
looking at the starlight
and something happened wav ng backwards
words
feather
spring
everyone wants the shine to last forever
how very brave
the first in a line packed away
into yellow leather cases on arrival
best not enquire the origins
of some of these strange skins
cut into strips or folded into collars
your voice needs to start low
go high
and go back down again
you're hesitating

trois types d'operation de voix
tricotine
velour de laine
poult de soie
if they ask you to jig
tell them where to go
remove your gloves
before
indicating your mouth with the thumb
in a repetitive gesture
this is an affectionate alternative for
I don't know I don't care
you shrug with this one
no it's like a tutting sound
as if you were sucking your teeth
more desirable
and harder to get
I saw your shape at forty paces
at five your mouth
at none your conversation
a face can cost you
sometimes in captions
sometimes in odd remarks
hello
our dancing has slowed down
you cuckoo
shouting all day at no-one
but you looked wonderful
scrawled across the floor the other night
almost real
even down to a single swear word
where there is nothing there is something
surprised
you illuminate the air beside your face
not in the sky
one star
but in your hair
difficult to gauge
and dangerous to repeat
the world one might meet
on a walk in the street
dawdling in its tracks

and simultaneously skipping a decade
another arcade has crashed
and I'm not afraid of losing it
highly cut
I look at you with half-closed eyes
there is a beauty in the pattern of your shadows
a memorial you could hardly have desired
firmly-worded
the carapace-like infrastructure
of your every word
without sibilants
despite the S-curve of your spine
moved in space
if the interspace were empty
by an impact
a part in the production of hearing
against something else
filled with air
say
the soul is a magnitude
like that of number
how
indifferently of its parts
or in the sense of a point
if a point can be called apart
position and motion
grow in both directions
having the power to perceive
and the sense itself divisible
in being
numerically undivided as well
as we can distinguish
while not existing
separate from sensible
or in definition
for everything is moved
by pushing and pulling
stopping for breathing
what has been said
in different lights
in a material
described by another

against destruction
by wind rain and heat
as stones bricks and timbers
say that it is what moves
the body so
is a body organized
a certain kind of object
which has no single name
imagine must be a move
meant sweet from hot
called appetite
is clear
this description
holds only
yet your life as it looked when you met it first
as beautiful and rarely seen
outside in its everyday intercourse
yet difficult
a shrinking
subject to trials of no conception
is it new
does it work
is it yours
ideas wanting
in the dressing and the fitting
styles draw lines
within things themselves
illusion of a class already
how blind is your audience
written for less this desire does not stick to itself
prettiness is not a rent
you pay for occupying a space
begin to walk
p's and q's can make a word unbalanced
frock
moist
my favourite word is haberdasher
that's moot
curated
gamine
eponymous
irregardless is not a word

articulate
breaking a window
coagulate and lubricant
dropped on the floor
peering into your handbag
to take pictures
hat lost
you have a handkerchief
but there are not that many hollyhocks
you iron though there is nothing left to iron
testing hell cigarette in hand
bless your cotton stockings
and your legs uncrossed
giving birth to a bunch of roses
eating the last bun left in the music box
I will make you a new hat
with the feathers from last night's dinner
and when I say entertain
I mean entertain
you jumped so fast
your skirt caught fire
applying rouge
your disembodied head and hands
negotiate in no man's land
the gloved one holds the compact
watch your step
if you mistake
your bones will make
guns and planes
and tanks and ships and ammunition
run around the edge to check the shape
what type of curve are you
balancing difficulty on one foot
in interminable circles a sudden thought
slap bang
thin walls slide
the varying tension of skins balancing
on the balls of your eyes
bend forward
step through
thrum
and sort out where to sit

assume speech on that spot
so like all night
surrounding targets
pull away from the sides
and peel into the summerhouse
facility of elocution
working in the surface department
assembling a section of the leading edge
here today
should be so sounded
as to not tomorrow
the extreme falling
inflection
as at the absolute end of a subject
when the grammar is complete
and the thought yet incomplete
is it white or black
in the middle of a complicated sentence
music in the accent
becomes less and less important
the more oratorical you become
for but
read that
hauteur
come-hither
high-cut

.

www.ingramcontent.com/pod-product-compliance
Lightning Source LLC
Chambersburg PA
CBHW070756050426
42449CB00010B/2501